Complete Insider's Off-the-Beaten-Path Experience (Includes Villa d'Este and Villa Adriana Tour)

Lazio, Tivoli

Travel Guide
2023

Curtis Kerr

All Rights Reserved!

No part of this book may be reproduced, stored in a retrieval system, or transmitted in any form or by any means, electronic, mechanical, photocopying, recording, or otherwise, without the prior written permission of the copyright owner.

Copyright 2023, Curtis Kerr.

Table of Contents

INTRODUCTION

Welcome to Lazio Region

Tuscany, Umbria, Marche, Abruzzo, Molise, and Campania are all borders of the fascinating region of Lazio, which is situated in central Italy. Rome is unquestionably the region's crown gem, but Lazio has much more to offer than its well-known capital. It has a varied landscape that skillfully combines historical monuments, scenic farmland, and breathtaking coastline regions.

There was a feeling of expectation in the air as I exited the train in Tivoli. I was eager to learn more about this mysterious village hidden in Lazio, Italy, after hearing rumors about it. I was enticed to go on and go on an off-the-beaten-path journey by the streets' enticing light.

I was in awe of the quaint buildings that were festooned with vibrant flowers as I strolled along the little cobblestone alleyways. Tivoli, remote from the busy masses of Rome, possessed a genuine Italian charm. I had the impression that I was traveling through time with each step, taking in the fascinating history of this undiscovered treasure.

The Italian Renaissance masterpiece Villa d'Este was where I started. I was immediately mesmerized by the wealth and grandeur that enveloped me as soon as I entered the home. I was transported to another time by the elaborate frescoes, lavish courtyards, and gushing waterfalls. The perfectly designed gardens' splendor and the sound of swirling water and songbirds completely captivated me.

Next, I was greeted by the attraction of Villa Adriana, the hideaway that originally belonged to Emperor Hadrian. I gazed at the ruins of old buildings, the great halls, and the expansive gardens as I explored the immense complex.

I couldn't help but feel a strong connection to the past as each stone appeared to be speaking stories from a bygone period.

I realized Tivoli had taken a bit of my heart as the sun sank. This off-the-beaten-track encounter had shown me a side of Italy I had long wanted to see. I enthusiastically set off on my Tivoli trip, prepared to make lifelong memories in this lovely region of Lazio, with the promise of more undiscovered gems and genuine moments to follow.

Rome, the capital of Lazio, is a historic and culturally rich city. The Colosseum, the Roman Forum, the Pantheon, and Vatican City, with its famed St. Peter's Basilica and the Vatican Museums, are among the famous sites that draw large crowds of tourists. The lively ambiance, hopping piazzas, and delectable food of the city make it an alluring vacation spot.

Lazio has attractive villages and cities that entice their appeal outside of Rome. The magnificent Villa d'Este and Villa Adriana, both listed as UNESCO World Heritage monuments, are located in the hilltop hamlet of Tivoli. These incredible homes transport guests through time with their stunning gardens, ornate fountains, and amazing architecture.

The undulating hills, vineyards, and olive groves of the Lazio countryside provide a tranquil respite from the bustle of the city. Cities like Viterbo, renowned for its hot springs and ancient architecture, and the charming town of Calcutta, built on a tuff cliff, provide a taste of a more sedate, traditional Italy.

The coastal regions of Lazio are very attractive. Sperlonga, Gaeta, and Sabaudia are delightful coastal villages with lovely beaches that are ideal for leisurely holidays.

Indulge in mouthwatering seafood, relax on fine sand beaches, and explore the many Roman ruins that dot the coastline.

Lazio provides a varied and enthralling experience for visitors looking for a classic Italian adventure, whether they like to immerse themselves in the grandeur of Rome, find undiscovered treasures in little villages, or take in the natural beauty of the countryside and sea.

Tivoli: A Hidden Gem Uncovered

Tivoli is a hidden treasure just waiting to be found, perched amid the lovely Lazio hills. While Rome often steals the show, this charming hamlet provides a welcome break from the throng and a chance to see a lesser-known Italian destination's true beauty.

Intensely beautiful and historically significant, Tivoli is a location where every turn offers a tale from the past. Its cobblestone alleys snake through historic districts, surrounded by colorful homes decorated with blossoming flowers, making each turn a picture-perfect spectacle. Visitors may get a closer-knit and more laid-back view of Italy because of the little town's intimate size and slower pace.

But Tivoli shines because of the town's treasures. The architectural wonders Villa d'Este and Villa Adriana have gained their status as UNESCO World Heritage sites.

The Italian Renaissance masterpiece Villa d'Este mesmerizes guests with its lavish interiors, stunning gardens, and intricate fountains that appear to come to life with each whimsical water show. It's a location where it's simple to become lost in a serene and beautiful environment.

Travelers may travel to ancient Rome by visiting Villa Adriana, also known as Hadrian's Villa. This enormous structure, which previously functioned as Emperor Hadrian's retreat, provides an insight into the luxury and magnificence of the Roman Empire. Visitors may awe at the elaborately carved buildings, stunning sculptures, and expansive gardens that were once enjoyed by the emperor himself by seeing the remains.

Beyond these well-known locations, Tivoli has many more surprises in store for the adventurous tourist. Its meandering lanes lead to secret squares, quaint cafés, and neighborhood markets where one may sample the local cuisine. Visitors are encouraged to wander slowly, take in the scenery, and interact with the friendly residents by the town's warm and welcoming attitude.

The appeal of Tivoli rests in its capacity to take tourists back in time while providing a close-up view of the real Italian way of life. This location combines history, art, and nature to provide a memorable experience. Tivoli is a hidden jewel that promises to enthrall and create a lasting impact for anyone looking for a genuine off-the-beaten-path trip.

Why Visit the Lazio Region?

The year offers a wealth of persuasive reasons to start on an amazing visit to the Lazio area, including Tivoli. Here are a few alluring elements that contribute to its value as a travel destination:

Rome, the eternal city famed for its incomparable historical and cultural assets, is located in the Lazio region and has a rich historical and cultural heritage. Rome provides a magnificent immersion into ancient history and famous art, from the splendor of the Colosseum to the majesty of the Vatican City.

You may follow in the footsteps of emperors and see the remains of a strong civilization by exploring the area.

Lazio provides unique experiences of Italian culture outside of the busy metropolis. Particularly Tivoli is a jewel that offers an authentic Italian experience away from the tourists. Visitors may immerse themselves in the local culture and taste the genuine flavors of the area thanks to its gorgeous streets, neighborhood markets, and traditional food.

Off-the-Beaten-Path Exploration: While Rome draws millions of tourists each year, exploring Lazio's less-traveled areas offers the potential to find undiscovered gems. With the Villa d'Este and Villa Adriana, Tivoli provides a unique experience where you may be in awe of the stunning architecture, stroll through gorgeous gardens, and interact with the area's historical past.

Natural Beauty & Scenic Landscapes: Lazio's diversified geography includes beautiful rural and coastal regions in addition to its ancient towns. For leisurely drives and beautiful treks, the area's undulating hills, vineyards, and olive orchards provide a magnificent background. Lazio's coastal cities also provide beautiful beaches, glistening waves, and spectacular vistas that are ideal for unwinding and recuperation.

Lazio organizes several festivals and events all year long, allowing visitors to appreciate regional customs and take in the energetic spirit of the area. These cultural events, which range from religious processions to music festivals, provide fascinating insights into the history and traditions of the Lazio area.

Travelers may expect to discover a unique combination of historical marvels, real-world adventures, and stunning scenery throughout

Lazio, including Tivoli. This area of Italy has something to offer any tourist, whether they are looking for historical history, gastronomic treats, or natural beauty. It's a chance to go above and beyond the traditional tourist experience and enjoy the true spirit of Italy.

II. GETTING TO TIVOLI

How to Get to Tivoli

Tivoli, an Italian city in the Lazio region, is close to several transit hubs. Here are various ways to get to Tivoli:

Rail: Tivoli is easily accessible by rail, which makes it a practical means of transportation. From Roma Termini, Rome's primary railway station, trains leave frequently. Depending on the kind of train used, it takes between 30 and 1 hour to go from Rome to Tivoli. It is wise to research train timetables beforehand and buy tickets either in person at the station or online.

Bus: Between Rome and Tivoli, there are bus services that run. The bus ride normally lasts one hour, however, this might change depending on the flow of traffic. In Rome, buses often leave from Tiburtina Station or different locations across the city. It is advised to look into the bus timetables and ticket availability in advance.

Car: Driving allows you the freedom to explore the surrounding places at your speed and makes it simple to get to Tivoli. You may travel the A24 or A1 freeways from Rome to Tivoli, depending on your starting point. Depending on the amount of traffic, the trip might take up to an hour. Parking spaces are available at Tivoli, however, it's best to research parking possibilities beforehand.

Private Transfers: You may also book a cab or organize a private transport from Rome to Tivoli. This offers flexibility and convenience, particularly if you have tight deadlines or want a more specialized level of service. Private transfers may be scheduled via several transportation providers or directly with your lodging.

Once at Tivoli, you may walk about and explore the town since it is very small. However, you could think about taking local buses or taxis if you want to get to the Villa d'Este and Villa Adriana, which are a little beyond the town center.

To guarantee a pleasant and trouble-free journey to Tivoli, it is advised to check the most recent transit schedules, ticket pricing, and any COVID-19-related instructions before your departure.

Directions from Rome & Other Major Cities

By Train: You may go to Tivoli from Rome by taking a train from Roma Termini, the city's primary railway station. Depending on the kind of train, the trip might take anywhere from 30 minutes to an hour. Trains leave often. Purchase tickets at the station or online after consulting the train timetables. You may easily go to the town center on foot or by local bus after arriving at Tivoli station.

By Car: If you want to drive, you may take the A24 motorway from Rome to Tivoli. Leave Rome and go down the A24 in the direction of Tivoli. Depending on the amount of traffic, the trip normally takes 30 to 1 hour. When you arrive in Tivoli, follow the directions to the town center or your intended location.

Location from other Major cities:

You may catch a train from Florence's Santa Maria Novella station to Roma Termini if you're coming from Florence. It takes the train 1.5 to 2 hours to get there. To get to Tivoli from Rome Termini, follow the above-mentioned routes.

From Naples: Take a train from Napoli Centrale station to Roma Termini to go to Tivoli from

Naples. It takes between 1 hour and 10 minutes and 2 hours to go by rail. Once you get to Roma Termini, use the already indicated guidelines to go to Tivoli.

You should be aware that these are just approximate instructions and that actual journey times may vary according to traffic, train timetables, and other circumstances. To ensure a smooth and effective trip to Tivoli, it is always advisable to check the most recent transportation options, schedules, and any applicable travel restrictions or guidelines before your departure.

Tivoli Transportation Options

Buses are the main mode of public transit in Tivoli, and they provide easy access to the town's many sights and districts. Here is a list of Tivoli's available public transportation options:

Local Buses: Major tourist destinations like Villa d'Este and Villa Adriana are easily accessible throughout Tivoli thanks to its dependable local bus system. The bus stations are well-signposted, and the buses often operate on time. At the bus stations or the Tivoli tourist information office, you may obtain bus routes and timetables. It is advised that you check the timetables beforehand and make your travel arrangements appropriately.

Shuttle Buses: During the busiest travel times, there may be shuttle buses that are designed exclusively for tourists going to Villa d'Este and Villa Adriana. These shuttles provide a practical method to get to the sites without having to worry about parking or getting lost in the city. You may ask at your hotel or the tourist information center for information on shuttle services.

Walking: The town center of Tivoli is small and conveniently accessible, enabling tourists to experience the majority of the top sights and historical locations on foot. Because the streets are pedestrian-friendly, you may explore the town on foot while taking in its atmosphere and finding hidden treasures.

It's important to keep in mind that public transit alternatives might change or vary, particularly during holidays or in cases of unanticipated events. Before your visit, it's a good idea to see if there have been any updates or changes to the bus timetables, routes, or other transit options. The most recent information on public transit alternatives in Tivoli may be found at the tourist information center.

III. EXPLORING TIVOLI

Overview of the Neighborhoods and Districts in Tivoli:

Tivoli, a lovely town in Italy's Lazio region, is well-known for its outstanding ancient structures as well as its many neighborhoods and districts, each of which has its distinctive character and charms. Here is a detailed description of Tivoli's districts and neighborhoods, including information on what makes each one interesting to explore:

Tivoli Historic core: The town's beating heart, Tivoli's historic core is a charming tangle of winding lanes, charming plazas, and brightly painted buildings festooned with flowers. You may sample genuine Italian food in the charming cafés, neighborhood stores, and classic trattorias you'll come across while strolling around this region. The magnificent Duomo di Tivoli, a stunning cathedral from the 11th century, can also be found in the old town.

Villa d'Este: The famed Villa d'Este, a UNESCO World Heritage site, is located in the Villa d'Este district, just outside the old center. This region is marked by gorgeous Renaissance buildings, lush gardens, and intricate fountains. You may enjoy the villa's splendor and wealth, as well as the beauty of its flowing water features, by exploring the neighborhood.

Villa Adriana: The enormous remains of Villa Adriana, also known as Hadrian's Villa, are found in the Villa Adriana neighborhood, which is not far from the heart of Tivoli. This enormous archaeological site offers insight into the opulent lifestyle of Emperor Hadrian as well as the magnificence of ancient Roman architecture. Wandering about the ruins, admiring the perfectly maintained buildings, and taking in the tranquil atmosphere of the surroundings are all possible when exploring the area.

The Bagni di Tivoli neighborhood, which is outside of Tivoli, is renowned for its hot baths and spa facilities. You may indulge in treatments and unwind in the healing waters in this region, which provides a peaceful haven. The gorgeous scenery and the Aniene River, which are both located in Bagni di Tivoli, provide possibilities for outdoor pursuits like hiking and picnics.

Monti Tiburtini: Perched on a hilltop above Tivoli, Monti Tiburtini provides breathtaking views of the city and its surroundings. The lovely private lanes and houses in this neighborhood serve as its defining features. You may experience the tranquility of the hills, stunning landscapes, and a tranquil atmosphere while exploring Monti Tiburtini.

You'll not only come across the major sights as you stroll through these Tivoli neighborhoods and districts, but you'll also get the chance to find undiscovered nooks, meet welcoming locals, and experience the true Italian atmosphere. Every location has a unique tale to share, which gives your total Tivoli experience more depth and richness.

Must-see Sights and Attractions

Tivoli, a charming town in Italy's Lazio region, is well known for its outstanding monuments and attractions. When touring Tivoli, the following locations have to be on your itinerary:

Villa d'Este is a spectacular Renaissance mansion that is home to gorgeous gardens and ornate fountains. It is a UNESCO World Heritage site. Take a stroll around the lushly planted tiered gardens and take in the elaborate water elements that give this location its true beauty.

Visit the remains of Villa Adriana (Hadrian's Villa), the opulent hideaway of Emperor Hadrian, on the outskirts of Tivoli. Discover the huge complex, which shows the amazing architecture, including temples, palaces, theaters, and spas. This ancient site will capture your mind with its fine intricacies and historical importance.

Rocca Pia: Rocca Pia is a historic fortification that dominates the town's skyline and provides sweeping views of Tivoli and its surroundings. Learn about its history and take in the expansive views from the top of the fortress walls by going on a guided tour.

Temple of Vesta: This well-preserved Roman temple, which dates to the first century BC, is situated in the middle of Tivoli's historic district. Imagine the ancient rites that previously took place within the walls of this beautiful circular edifice while you admire it.

Visit the Duomo di Tivoli, the town's principal cathedral, which has a fusion of Romanesque and Gothic architectural elements. Step inside to enjoy its magnificent design and possibly join a service to feel the spiritual environment.

Villa Gregoriana: A tranquil getaway with rich vegetation, gorges, and waterfalls, Villa Gregoriana is a natural park. Take a stroll along the trails, passing across historic bridges and taking in the peace of nature.

Explore the Roman temple known as the Temple of the Sibyl, which is located atop Tivoli's acropolis. The temple, while in ruins, is nonetheless a striking reminder of Tivoli's historical past.

Visit the Roman temple named the Sanctuary of Hercules Victor, which is devoted to the mythical hero. Take in the calm environment and well-restored columns at this historic location.

These places of interest and famous buildings in Tivoli weave together a rich tapestry of the city's past, present, and future. Each location offers a distinctive viewpoint on the town's history, enabling you to immerse yourself in it while making priceless memories.

Best Time to Visit Tivoli

Depending on your choices and the experiences you're looking for, there is no one optimum time to visit Tivoli. Due to its Mediterranean environment, Tivoli has scorching summers and moderate winters. For each season, take into account the following:

Spring (April to June): The best time to visit Tivoli is in the spring. The weather is good, with moderate to warm temperatures. The grounds of Villa d'Este are bursting with color and scent thanks to the current bloom. It's a terrific time for outdoor exploration since there are fewer people around than at the height of summer.

Summer (July to August): Tivoli has warm, sunny weather throughout the summer, with the hottest months being July and August. Especially during the European summer vacation season, this is the busiest travel period. Be prepared for bigger crowds, especially around prominent sights like Villa d'Este and Villa Adriana. Summer may be a thrilling time to come if you don't mind the heat and appreciate the bustling environment.

Autumn (September to November): The lovely weather in the autumn makes it a good time to visit Tivoli. Both the temperature and the people are beginning to drop down. The gardens and the area's foliage take on lovely red, orange, and gold tones, making for a magnificent background for your travels.

Winter (December to February): Tivoli's winters are generally pleasant, with chilly temperatures and sporadic rain. During this time, the town has a calmer, more serene atmosphere, making it a fantastic opportunity to experience the sights without the crowds. It's crucial to be aware that certain locations, like Villa d'Este, can have fewer operating hours in the winter.

Check the neighborhood events calendar as well, since Tivoli organizes several festivals and events all year round that may enhance your trip with even more cultural immersion.

The ideal time to go to Tivoli ultimately depends on your particular interests. Tivoli provides something special in every season, regardless of whether you enjoy beautiful weather, vivid gardens, or a calmer ambiance.

IV. VILLA D'ESTE: A MASTERPIECE OF ITALIAN RENAISSANCE

History and Significance Villa d'este

The spectacular Renaissance estate known as Estate d'Este is situated in Tivoli, Italy, and is famed for its stunning gardens and intricate fountains. Villa d'Este, which dates back to the 16th century, is very significant historically and culturally. Here is a summary of its background and significance:

- **Construction and Cardinal Ippolito d'Este:** Cardinal Ippolito II d'Este, a member of the illustrious d'Este family and the grandson of Pope Alexander VI commissioned the construction of the villa, which was meant to be a lavish residence befitting the cardinal's prestigious status.

- **Architectural Mastery:** Pirro Ligorio, a well-known architect of the period, is credited with creating the Villa d'Este's stunning exterior and interior designs.

- With its imposing exterior, breathtaking courtyards, and graceful internal spaces, the house exemplifies a combination of Renaissance and Mannerist styles.

- **Gardens and Fountains:** The Villa d'Este's gardens and fountains are its greatest wonders. The cardinal turned the environment into a magnificent work of art after visiting the Villa Adriana ruins for inspiration. The gardens' terraces, walkways, and lush vegetation contribute to the tranquil environment. The enormous system of fountains, which has more than 500 jets, cascades, and waterfalls, is the most prominent aspect. The water in these fountains flows naturally utilizing gravity thanks to an inventive hydraulic design.

- Villa d'Este is a site that has been recognized by UNESCO as a World Heritage Site. It was honored for its extraordinary cultural significance because it embodies the best of Italian Renaissance garden engineering and architecture.

- **Cultural Influence:** The architecture and landscape design of Europe have been greatly influenced by Villa d'Este. Numerous garden designs around Europe, notably the renowned gardens of Versailles in France, were influenced by its creative use of water and landscape features.

Today, Villa d'Este draws tourists from all over the globe who come to gaze at its majestic beauty and take in its ancient atmosphere. Visitors are still mesmerized by the gardens and fountains, which provide a window into the opulent way of life of the Renaissance.

The Villa d'Este is a prime example of the Renaissance's outstanding aesthetic and architectural achievements. A must-see site for everyone traveling through Tivoli or the Lazio area, it is a genuine treasure of cultural heritage thanks to the natural blending of nature and water components and its rich history.

The Villa's Architectural and Design

The Villa d'Este is recognized for its extraordinary architecture and design, which highlights the Renaissance era's creative genius. Here are some of the villa's architectural and design highlights:

- **Magnificent Façade:** The villa's magnificent façade is symmetrically designed and has rows of balconies and arched windows. The use of pilasters and ornate motifs gives the façade a feeling of grandeur and elegance.

- **Courtyards and Loggias:** Villa d'Este is home to lovely courtyards and loggias that provide breathtaking vistas and relaxing areas. These outdoor spaces showcase the expertise of Renaissance architecture with beautiful arches, columns, and finely carved embellishments.

- **Interior Spaces:** The Villa d'Este's interior is similarly stunning, with exquisitely furnished chambers that capture the opulent way of life of the Renaissance period. A lavish ambiance is created by elaborate frescoes, dexterous stucco work, and beautiful ceilings decorated with paintings and gold leaf.

- **Terraced grounds:** The villa's grounds are arranged in many terraces, resulting in a stunning environment. Each terrace provides a distinctive viewpoint and special amenities including walkways, gardens, and lounging places that are encircled by colorful flowers and lush vegetation.

- The Fountain of the Organ is a magnificent example of hydraulic engineering and one of Villa d'Este's most recognizable features. Visitors to this unusual fountain may enjoy a multisensory experience because of the mechanical organ that it features.

- The Fountain of the Hundred Fountains is a noteworthy addition to the area. This enormous fountain is made up of a long wall covered in innumerable little fountains, which together provide a captivating watery symphony. It is a convincing illustration of the creativity and skill of Renaissance hydraulic engineering.

Visitors may see a variety of sculptures and statues, including mythical characters, deities, and historical individuals, all across the grounds. These pieces of art give the villa's décor a sense of timeless beauty and narrative appeal.

The harmony, balance, and elegance of the Renaissance are reflected in the architecture and design of Villa d'Este. A trip back in time to the luxury and aesthetic magnificence of the Renaissance is made possible by the building's beautiful façade, superb internal spaces, attractive gardens, and inventive water systems.

Exploring The Breathtaking Gardens and Fountains

Visitor immersion in the beauty and inventiveness of Renaissance architecture is created by exploring the magnificent gardens and fountains of Villa d'Este. What to anticipate when you enter the gardens is as follows:

- The gardens of Villa d'Este are arranged on a series of terraces, resulting in a beautiful fusion of architecture and nature. You'll be treated to breathtaking vistas of the surroundings and the town of Tivoli as you climb through the terraces.

- A profusion of beautiful flora, including clipped hedges, well-kept lawns, and towering trees, adorns the grounds. The lush, well-kept greenery creates a tranquil, rejuvenating atmosphere that beckons guests to stroll and explore the garden's secret nooks.

- Meandering paths and walkways take you around the gardens and direct you to various locations and focus points. Enjoy the beauty of your surroundings as you walk casually along these trails surrounded by vibrant flowers and scented blooming.

- The ornate fountains that embellish different areas of the landscape are without a doubt the gardens' main attraction. Over 500 water elements, including jets, cascades, and waterfalls, are powered by a complex hydraulic system at the Villa d'Este.
As you see water dancing and sparkling in the sun, be in awe of the technical prowess of the Renaissance.

- Fountain of the Organ: Experience the confluence of water and music at the famous Fountain of the Organ. Incorporating a mechanical organ, this fountain produces lovely melodies as water runs past it, giving a unique and hypnotic sensory experience.

- Fountain of the Hundred Fountains: The Gardens' Fountain of the Hundred Fountains is another breathtaking sight. It generates a sensory-appealing water symphony because of its abundance of little fountains. Spend a minute admiring the workmanship and complexity of this enormous fountain.

- Discover secret grottoes and nymph sculptures dotted across the grounds in "Grottoes and Nymphs." These mythological characters give the whole design a little magic and narrative, inspiring awe and interest.

- Calm Seating Places: As you explore the grounds, you will come across calm seating places that have been thoughtfully positioned. Relax for a minute, take in the scenery, and consider how beautiful Villa d'Este is.

Discovering the Villa d'Este's gardens and fountains is a voyage of sensual enjoyment and artistic admiration. You can see how art and nature can coexist peacefully, as well as how engineering from the Renaissance was innovative. Get ready to be mesmerized by the serene beauty and classic elegance these gardens and fountains offer.

V. Villa Adriana: The Emperor's Retreat

Overview of Villa Adriana (Hadrian's Villa)

The remarkable archaeological site known as Villa Adriana, commonly referred to as Hadrian's Villa, is situated near Tivoli, Italy. Built-in the second century AD, this vast structure served as Emperor Hadrian's opulent retreat and imperial home. Villa Adriana, one of the most spectacular and well-preserved Roman ruins, provides a fascinating look into the lavish way of life of the aristocracy in ancient Rome.

Villa Adriana was built during the era of Emperor Hadrian, who controlled the Roman Empire from 117 to 138 AD, and as such is of great historical value. Hadrian was well renowned for his appreciation of the arts and architecture, and he built this opulent home to showcase his wide range of passions as well as to demonstrate his dominance and fortune.

Architectural Wonder: The villa complex is spread out over 120 hectares and features a broad variety of architectural influences and styles. Villa Adriana's architectural style was influenced by features from Egyptian, Greek, and Roman civilizations, creating a unique synthesis of architectural forms.

Diverse Structures: Throughout Villa Adriana, you'll find a variety of buildings and structures that originally had a variety of uses. These facilities, which include palaces, temples, theaters, hot baths, libraries, and gardens, were all created to provide the emperor with an opulent and private getaway away from the bustle of Rome.

Greek and Egyptian Influences: The use of Greek and Egyptian architectural elements is one of Villa Adriana's standout characteristics. The Maritime Theater is a circular building with a center island that evokes Greek theaters, while the Canopus is a pool encircled by columns and sculptures that mimics the design of Egyptian temples.

Gardens & Landscaping: The villa's grounds are embellished with lovely gardens, terraces with magnificent landscaping, and water features. These features were put together to create a tranquil and scenic atmosphere, complete with rich vegetation, moving water, and peaceful vistas that served as the setting for the emperor's leisure pursuits and introspection.

UNESCO World Heritage Site: In 1999, Villa Adriana received the honor of being named a UNESCO World Heritage site in recognition of its exceptional global importance. The website exhibits the impressive architectural accomplishments of the Roman Empire and offers insightful information on the way of life and preferences of Roman emperors.

You may go back in time and experience the splendor and refinement of the Roman Empire by visiting Villa Adriana. For history buffs, lovers of architecture, and anybody trying to solve the riddles of ancient Rome, the site's many architectural styles, enormous ruins, and lush surroundings make it a must-visit location.

The Villa's History and Background

The architectural wonder known as Villa Adriana, commonly referred to as Hadrian's Villa, was built in the second century AD during the reign of Emperor Hadrian. A deeper look at the context and history of this exquisite home is provided below:

- Construction of Villa Adriana was ordered in the early second century AD by Emperor Hadrian, who was well-known for his love of building and frequent travels. The house was designed to be his lavish escape from Rome's political issues and a representation of his wide range of interests and aesthetic preferences.

- **Location**: In the gorgeous Lazio countryside, some 30 kilometers east of Rome, sits Tivoli, where Villa Adriana may be found. The location was carefully selected because of its advantageous setting on the Tiburtine Hills' slopes, which provided stunning views of the surroundings.

- **Influences on architecture:** The villa's design was influenced by several ancient civilizations since Hadrian was well known for his respect for diverse cultures and civilizations. Greek, Egyptian, and Roman architectural elements were used to create a distinctive synthesis that displayed the emperor's varied preferences.

- The villa was enlarged and altered throughout Hadrian's rule into a vast structure that spanned more than 120 hectares. It was a self-contained realm with many buildings, structures, gardens, and water features that suited the emperor's requirements.

- A luxury retreat for the emperor and his court, Villa Adriana also served as a source of ideas for Hadrian's construction endeavors. He was able to entertain visitors, engage in intellectual activities, and get away from the stresses of the capital city at the house. Additionally, it was used as a test site for architectural concepts that would eventually guide the construction of other colossal structures around the empire.

- **Decline and Rediscovery:** Following Hadrian's death, the villa began to deteriorate. Over the years, it was pillaged, neglected, and damaged by natural calamities. Villa Adriana wasn't rediscovered or its importance realized until the Renaissance era. Since then, work has been done to excavate and preserve the site, enabling visitors to see the villa's opulence in its current state.

Emperor Hadrian's vision, ingenuity, and magnificence are shown through Villa Adriana. Its distinctive architectural design, substantial ruins, and exquisitely planted surroundings provide an insight into the opulent way of life of the Roman aristocracy. It continues to wow tourists with its historical and cultural value as one of Italy's most significant ancient sites.

Key Features and Structures within the Complex

The vast Villa Adriana complex has several significant elements and constructions that highlight the site's magnificent architecture. When you explore the villa, you may find the following noteworthy features:

- **Canopus and Serapeum:** Reminiscent of an Egyptian temple, the Canopus is a large rectangular lake encircled by columns and sculptures. It has the name of the Canopus, an ancient Egyptian metropolis. The Serapeum, a little circular structure devoted to the Egyptian deity Serapis, sits nearby.

Maritime Theater: The Maritime Theater is a circular building encircled by a moat and featuring a central island. It is said that the emperor utilized it as a getaway and amusement location. A bridge led to the island, which offered a peaceful area for reflection and recreation.

- The Golden Square, also known as Piazza d'Oro, was an opulent patio with golden accents. It served as the focal point for social and ceremonial gatherings and displayed the villa's luxury and grandeur.

- **Imperial Palace:** The Imperial Palace was the focal point of the villa community and served as Emperor Hadrian's imperial home. It was made up of several linked structures, including reception areas, individual residences, and office buildings. The castle included apartments, courtyards, and gardens that were lavishly furnished.

- **Greek Theater:** The semi-circular Greek Theater at Villa Adriana is carved out of a hillside. It could hold a sizable crowd and was utilized for theatrical performances. The theater displays how Greek architecture influenced Hadrian's architectural decisions.

- **Libraries**: The many libraries of the Villa Adriana were a testament to Hadrian's passion for study and knowledge. These libraries were places for study, reflection, and intellectual activities and had significant book collections.

Thermal Baths: The villa complex included several thermal baths, displaying the Romans' love of leisure, well-being, and health. These spas had heated pools, hot and cold chambers, and complex heating systems.

Villa Adriana was noted for its luxuriant gardens and beautifully designed grounds. Fountains, water features, sculptures, and well-kept paths were all included in the gardens. They offered peaceful areas for introspection, strolls, and aesthetic pleasure.

Visitors may see the variety and beauty of ancient Roman architecture by touring Villa Adriana. The diverse architecture of the complex, which includes Egyptian-inspired features as well as opulent palaces and theaters, provides insights into the opulent way of life and cultural influences of Emperor Hadrian. Discovering the splendor of Villa Adriana is a unique and immersive experience made possible by each building within the complex.

VI. OFF-THE-BEATEN-PATH EXPERIENCES IN TIVOLI

Lesser-known Attractions and Hidden Gems

The most well-known sights in Tivoli are Villa d'Este and Villa Adriana, but there are also many lesser-known sites and undiscovered jewels that are well worth seeing. These off-the-beaten-track locations provide an opportunity to dive deeper into the region's rich history and culture. Here is a detailed guide to some of these undiscovered treasures:

- **Santuario di Ercole Vincitore**: This historic shrine is close to Villa Adriana and honors Hercules Victor, the Roman deity of might and triumph. Discover the holy site's remnants, which feature a massive altar and a circular temple, to learn more about the ancient Romans' religious traditions.

- **Villa Gregoriana** is a peaceful park that provides a welcome respite from the busy metropolis. It is tucked away in a verdant ravine. Discover secret waterfalls as you meander along the meandering roads and take in the breathtaking natural splendor of the surroundings. The Temple of Vesta and the Temple of the Sibyl are among the historic monuments in the park.

- **Rocca Pia:** Visit Rocca Pia, a medieval fortification built on a hilltop in Tivoli's historic district. Explore the quaint alleyways that encircle the fortress while taking a leisurely walk around the defensive walls and taking in the magnificent views of the city. Don't pass up the opportunity to visit the Museo della Città (City Museum), which is located within the Rocca and has relics that depict Tivoli's history.

- **Villa d'Este Gardens:** The gardens of Villa d'Este are frequently disregarded, even though their water features are famous. Spend some time strolling around the immaculately maintained grounds, which are embellished with lovely flowers, sculptures, and elegant paths. The grounds provide a tranquil setting and breathtaking views of the surroundings.

- **The Tempio delle Tosse** is a little-known example of Roman construction that may be seen close to Villa Gregoriana. The ruins of this little temple, which was built in honor of the goddess Tosse, provide some insight into earlier religious customs. Enjoy the quiet of the location while admiring the intricate architectural features of an older but less well-known building.

- Step into the majestic **Palazzo Rospigliosi** in the center of Tivoli and be amazed by the amazing paintings and sumptuous furnishings. The Casino dell'Aurora, a masterwork of Baroque art with murals by famous artist Guido Reni, is housed in Palazzo Rospigliosi. Explore the palace's beautiful chambers and grounds while taking in the rich intricacies of the paintings.

- Visit the quaint church, **Chiesa di San Biagio**, which is hidden in a peaceful area of Tivoli. The Chiesa di San Biagio, which was built in the ninth century, has a stunning Romanesque design. Enter to see its elaborate altar and tranquil atmosphere away from the hordes of the more well-known sights.

- **Ponte Gregoriano**: Cross this attractive bridge that crosses the Aniene River, the Ponte Gregoriano. Beautiful views of Villa Gregoriana and the natural surroundings are available from the bridge. Take some great pictures and time to enjoy the serenity of the river.

You may learn more about Tivoli's rich history, architecture, and natural beauty by exploring these lesser-known sites and hidden jewels there. Spend some time venturing off the beaten tourist trail to uncover the mysteries that are concealed inside Tivoli's streets and surroundings.

Authentic Dining Experiences and Local Cuisine

Visitors may enjoy a variety of unique eating experiences at Tivoli that let them explore the flavors of the regional cuisine. Here are some gastronomic highlights to check out, ranging from classic cuisine to regional specialties:

Porchetta: A tasty roast pig dish with Lazio area roots, porchetta is one of the most well-known street dishes in Italy. Take pleasure in flavorful slices of slow-roasted pork that are served on a loaf of crusty bread and seasoned with herbs and spices. To sample this tasty treat, look for local vendors or eateries that specialize in porchetta.

Cacio e Pepe: This traditional pasta dish from Rome has entered the Tivoli food scene. The name Cacio e Pepe, which means "cheese and pepper," accurately describes this simple but tasty dish made with spaghetti, Pecorino Romano cheese, and freshly ground black pepper. The recipe is a perfect illustration of the elegance of Italian simplicity and the use of premium ingredients.

Abbacchio alla Romana is a well-known Roman dish that features delicious and tender lamb. Usually, white wine, rosemary, and garlic are used to marinate the lamb before it is slowly cooked to perfection. It often includes roasted potatoes or artichokes, demonstrating the area's affinity for earthy tastes.

Pizza Romana: Indulge in a piece of real pizza made in Rome. Roman pizza often has a thin and crunchy crust, unlike Neapolitan pizza. Roman-style pizza, which may be topped with a variety of toppings including fresh mozzarella, tomatoes, and regional fruit, is a tasty and filling choice for a fast dinner.

Maritozzo: The maritozzo is a typical Roman pastry that you should indulge in if you want a sweet treat. It is a whipped cream-filled soft and sweet bun that is often eaten for breakfast or as a snack. For a lovely start to your day, serve it with a cup of coffee or cappuccino.

Tivoli is situated in the **Frascati wine area**, which is renowned for producing top-notch white wines. Enjoy the crisp flavors of a glass of Frascati wine, which is produced from Malvasia and Trebbiano grapes. Many neighborhood eateries provide a variety of regional wines to go with your meal.

Gelato: Having gelato is a must-do while visiting Italy, and Tivoli offers many gelaterias. Enjoy a few scoops of handcrafted gelato in a range of flavors, from traditional selections like pistachio and chocolate to more creative mashups. It's the ideal method for relieving heat and expressing your sweet craving.

Small trattorias, osterias, and family-run eateries that provide a more genuine and regional experience should be sought out while eating in Tivoli. These businesses often emphasize the use of local, seasonal foods and the preservation of traditional cooking methods. You may go on a savory adventure that honors the culinary customs of Tivoli and the Lazio area by learning about the regional food.

VII. EVENTS AND FESTIVALS IN TIVOLI

Annual Festivals and Cultural Events

Numerous festivals and cultural events are held in Tivoli every year to highlight the rich traditions, creative industries, and cultural legacy of the area. Attending these events is a wonderful opportunity to get immersed in the community and take in the vibrant ambiance of Tivoli. Mark the following important yearly festivals and events on your calendar:

- From June through September, the Tivoli Estate Festival (Estate Tivoli) presents a wide range of musical performances, theatrical productions, and films. There are performances staged all around the town, including the Rocca Pia, the Villa d'Este gardens, and other significant landmarks. The festival features a variety of creative forms and draws both domestic and foreign artists.

- Jazz lovers can schedule their trip around the Tivoli Jazz Festival, which usually takes place in July. Renowned jazz artists from Italy and throughout the globe come together for this festival to perform at several concerts, jam sessions, and seminars. Take in the soothing sounds of jazz at quaint locations all across the city.

- Festa di San Bartolomeo: The Festa di San Bartolomeo, which takes place on August 24th, is a religious event honoring Saint Bartholomew, the town's patron saint. The day begins with a somber Mass in the Chiesa di San Bartolomeo, which is followed by a jovial parade through Tivoli's streets that features music and traditional attire. Fireworks, food vendors, and cultural performances are all included during the celebration.

- Join in on the fun at the Tivoli Carnival, which, depending on the lunar calendar, takes place in either February or March. Tivoli's streets come alive with vibrant parades, ornate costumes, and upbeat music. It's a happy event that appeals to people of all ages and gives a look at the area's carnival customs.

- The annual Tivoli Arte Festival features several exhibits, installations, performances, and workshops to promote art and culture. It takes place in numerous locations, showcasing the creations of both regional and worldwide artists, such as museums, galleries, and public areas. In Tivoli, the festival encourages discussion and appreciation of modern art.

- The Tivoli Street Food Festival, which is usually held in late spring or early summer, is a must-attend event for foodies. The event brings together a broad range of food vendors serving delectable street cuisine specialties from many Italian regions and other countries. Enjoy a gourmet journey while sampling a variety of tastes and delicacies.

The calendar of Tivoli is made more vibrant and exciting by these yearly festivals and cultural events. They provide chances to interact with the neighborhood, observe traditions, and take in a variety of creative expressions. Check the particular dates and program information of these events before making travel plans to make sure you don't miss out on the one-of-a-kind experiences they provide.

Dates, Highlights and Local Traditions

The following list of yearly festivals and cultural events in Tivoli includes their dates, key features, and regional customs:

- **Tivoli Estate Festival (Estate Tivoli):**

June to September.
Highlights: Numerous venues, including the Villa d'Este Gardens and Rocca Pia, will host outdoor concerts, dance performances, theater productions, movie screenings, and art exhibits. A wide variety of creative abilities and cultural expressions are shown during the event.

- **Tivoli Jazz Festival:**

Time: July
Highlights: At concerts, jam sessions, and seminars, renowned jazz artists from Italy and other countries

play. The event creates a dynamic environment for jazz fans by bringing jazz's vivid sounds to Tivoli's attractive locations.

- **The Saint Bartholomew, Festival**

24th of August
Highlights: A religious event dedicated to Saint Bartholomew, Tivoli's patron saint. A Mass in the Chiesa di San Bartolomeo kicks off the celebrations, which are then followed by a vibrant parade through the streets that features traditional costumes, music, and fireworks. Food stands and cultural acts enhance the celebratory atmosphere.

- **Tivoli Carnival:**

Dates: Depending on the lunar calendar, February or March
Highlights: During the Tivoli Carnival, the streets come alive with colorful parades, elaborate

costumes, and jovial music. The event exhibits the local carnival customs and lets residents and guests alike get into the holiday mood.

- **Tivoli Art Festival:**

Dates: They change annually.
Highlights: Through exhibits, installations, performances, and workshops, this art festival honors contemporary art. In museums, galleries, and public settings, regional and international artists exhibit their works, promoting aesthetic appreciation and discussion.

- **Street Food Festival:**

At the end of spring or the beginning of summer
Highlights: The Tivoli Street Food Festival brings together food vendors that provide a broad variety of delectable street cuisine, making it a gourmet feast for food lovers. Discover a wide range of tastes

and delicacies from across the globe and various Italian regions.

Regional Customs:

- Traditional crafts like wood carving and mosaic creation have a long history in Tivoli. By visiting the studios and workshops of local artists, visitors may see these ancient techniques in action.

- The historical reenactments that take place at Tivoli, when inhabitants dress in period attire, are well-known. These recreations provide a window into the traditions and cultural history of Tivoli.

- The preparation of porchetta (roast pig) and other meals using seasonal, local ingredients are just a few examples of how deeply ingrained regional traditions are in Tivoli's local cuisine. You may discover the region's true tastes and culinary traditions by investigating the local food.

These important anniversaries, landmarks, and regional customs provide a look into Tivoli's thriving cultural landscape. To truly experience the town's festive and cultural atmosphere, make sure to research the precise dates and details of each event before your visit.

VIII. DAY TRIPS FROM TIVOLI

Explore the Nearby Towns and Attractions

Tivoli is an excellent starting point for seeing local cities and attractions because of its accessible location in the Lazio region. Here are some noteworthy day excursions from Tivoli that provide distinctive encounters and cultural learnings:

- **Rome**: The eternal city of Rome, which is not far from Tivoli, calls with its recognizable sights and extensive history. Discover well-known locations including the Spanish Steps, Vatican City's St. Peter's Basilica, the Roman Forum, and the Colosseum. Immerse yourself in the gastronomic delicacies, art, and culture of this historic city.

- Approximately 20 kilometers east of Tivoli lies the lovely village of **Subiaco**, which is tucked away in the Aniene Valley. Visit the revered Saint Benedict Monastery, a major pilgrimage destination that goes back to the sixth century. Visit the Rocca Abbaziale fortification, stroll through the quaint alleys of Subiaco, and take in the serene beauty of the surrounding landscape.

- **Castel Gandolfo** is a lovely village on the banks of Lake Albano that is well-known for being the papal summer palace. Take in the stunning views of the lake while seeing the Apostolic Palace and the town's historic district. Indulge in regional cuisine at one of the lakeside restaurants or take a leisurely walk around the waterfront.

- **Frascati** is a charming village that is well-known for its beautiful vineyards and top-notch white wine. Wander around the old town, see the Villa Aldobrandini and its lovely gardens, and partake in wine tastings at nearby vineyards. Porchetta is a typical dish from Frascati that you should try when you're there.

- **Palestrina**: Known for its historical and archaeological value, Palestrina is a town in the Monti Prenestini region. Visit the National Archaeological Museum, see the spectacular remains of the Sanctuary of Fortuna Primigenia, and meander through the old town's quaint medieval alleys. Don't pass up the chance to take in the expansive views from the Temple Terrace.

Despite being a part of Tivoli, Villa Adriana (also known as Hadrian's Villa) is a worthwhile day trip destination. This enormous archaeological site displays the splendor and extravagance of Emperor

Hadrian's retreat. Discover the palace, temple, and opulent garden ruins while admiring the brilliant architecture that exhibits the many influences of the Roman Empire.

These days, excursions from Tivoli provide a variety of experiences, including the chance to explore history and culture as well as the natural beauty and gastronomic pleasures. There is something around Tivoli for everyone, whether they are looking for historic sites, quaint villages, or a taste of the vibrant capital.

Suggested Itinerary for Day Trips

Here are three suggested day trip routes from Tivoli:

Exploring Rome
- Take a quick train trip from Tivoli to Rome in the morning.

- Spend the morning seeing Rome's historic attractions, including the Colosseum and Roman Forum.

- Eat a leisurely meal at a neighborhood trattoria while savoring genuine Roman fare.

- Visit Vatican City in the afternoon to see St. Peter's Basilica and tour the Vatican Museums, which include the world-famous Sistine Chapel.

- Explore Rome's ancient center on foot while stopping at famous sites including the Trevi Fountain, Pantheon, and Spanish Steps.

- Enjoy a great gelato to round off your day before taking the train back to Tivoli.

Lakeside Peace:

- Take a quick rail or bus from Tivoli to Castel Gandolfo to begin your day.

- Discover the Papal Palace and its lovely grounds while taking in the expansive views of Lake Albano.

- Take a leisurely boat trip on Lake Albano to unwind and take in the peace of the area.

- One of the exquisite eateries offers lakeside lunches where you may indulge in regional delicacies.

- Visit the adjacent village of Nemi, which is well-known for its strawberries and lovely lake, after lunch.

- Visit the Museum of Nemi Ships, which displays historic Roman naval vessels, and stroll around Nemi's charming streets.

- After spending the day relaxing by the lake, go back to Tivoli in the evening.

Journey Through Archaeology:
- Start your day off by taking a quick trip from Tivoli to Subiaco.

- Experience the history and spirituality of the Monastery of Saint Benedict by exploring it.

- Visit the breathtaking waterfalls of the Simbruini Mountains on a beautiful stroll through the lovely Aniene Valley.

- Enjoy a lunchtime picnic in the great outdoors while sampling regional specialties and goods.

- Travel to Palestrina in the afternoon to see the National Archaeological Museum and the Sanctuary of Fortuna Primigenia.

Enjoy a stroll around Palestrina's historic streets as you take in the quaint atmosphere and stunning scenery.

In the evening, return to Tivoli while thinking about the intriguing ancient sites and stunning scenery you saw throughout the day.

These itineraries provide a range of experiences, from seeing historic sites and Roman ruins to relaxing in lakeside villages and getting lost in the area's rich spiritual and archaeological legacy. Make the most of your day trip from Tivoli by selecting an itinerary that suits your interests and tastes.

IX. ACCOMMODATION OPTIONS IN TIVOLI

Tivoli's Lodging Choices And The Best Hotels

Tivoli has a variety of lodging choices to accommodate different needs and interests. The top hotels in Tivoli are listed below, along with a short description of each one:

1. Hotel Torre Sant'Angelo: This delightful hotel is housed in a historic structure and offers sweeping views of Tivoli. It is close to the Villa d'Este gardens. Modern conveniences are there, and the rooms are well-furnished. The hotel also boasts a lovely garden and patio where visitors may unwind and take in the view.

2. Palazzo Maggiore is a boutique hotel set in a restored 16th-century structure and is located in the center of Tivoli's old town. A combination of classic and modern elements is skillfully used to design the rooms. Visitors may take advantage of the breathtaking views from the rooftop deck.

3. The boutique hotel Hotel Cristallo Relais provides guests with a tranquil and unwinding stay in Tivoli. The rooms are roomy and well-appointed, with a blend of contemporary and traditional design. The hotel is perfectly situated close to Villa d'Este and other attractions, and it has a nice garden where guests may relax.

4. Villa Plauzi: A luxury getaway encircled by verdant gardens and vineyards, Villa Plauzi is tucked away in the countryside outside of Tivoli. The apartments are well-furnished and provide a relaxing ambiance. The hotel's outdoor pool, spa services, and an on-site restaurant offering delectable regional cuisine are all available to guests.

5. Hotel Le Rose: Located in a quiet residential neighborhood, Hotel Le Rose offers comfortable, welcoming lodging. Some of the comfortable, well-appointed rooms have views of the surrounding hills and are intimate. The hotel has a restaurant offering traditional Italian fare, and most of Tivoli's attractions are accessible on foot.

6. Hotel Sibilla: A family-run business with a friendly atmosphere, Hotel Sibilla is close to Villa Gregoriana and the Temple of Vesta. The hotel has a bar and a restaurant offering regional delicacies, and the rooms are cozy and attractively appointed. The property's garden and patio are also available for guests to use.

These Tivoli hotels provide a variety of facilities and attentive service to make your stay comfortable and pleasurable. There are alternatives to meet any traveler's preferences, whether you choose a historic structure in the center of the town or a tranquil refuge in the countryside.

X. PRACTICAL TRAVEL INFORMATION

Safety and Health Tips

Prioritizing safety and health is vital whether traveling to Tivoli or any other location. Following are some general health and safety recommendations:

- Research the current safety situation in Tivoli before your trip and keep up with any travel advice or recommendations given by the local government or the embassy or consulate of your country.

- Invest in travel insurance that will pay for unexpected costs like medical bills and trip cancellations. Be careful to study the fine print of the insurance and comprehend what is covered.

- Keep Your Things Safe: Always keep your items safe. Be vigilant about your surroundings, especially in busy places or on public transit, and keep valuables on hotel safes.

- Carry a water bottle with you and remember to remain hydrated, particularly in the summer when temperatures may soar. Make sure the tap water is safe to drink or use bottled water.

- Practice good hygiene by regularly washing your hands with soap and water or using hand sanitizer in the absence of handwashing facilities. Keep your hands away from your face, particularly if they aren't clean.

- Follow the COVID-19 recommendations: If you're traveling while the COVID-19 pandemic is active, abide by the recommendations and precautions made by the regional health authorities. This can include donning a mask, keeping a physical distance, and adhering to any particular admission rules or limits.

- Emergency Numbers: Become familiar with the regional emergency numbers for the police, fire, and medical services. In case of an emergency, have these numbers close at hand.

- Sun protection: Due to the bright weather in Tivoli, you should use sun protection. To protect oneself from UV radiation, put on sunscreen, a hat, and sunglasses.

- Respect Local Laws and Traditions: To ensure that you are courteous and conscious of cultural sensitivities, familiarize yourself with the local laws and traditions of Tivoli.

- If you need medical help while visiting Tivoli, get in touch with your hotel or the relevant authorities for advice. They may provide required support or point you in the direction of local medical services.

Keep in mind that these pointers are broad recommendations, so it's important to modify them to your circumstances and heed any further guidance given by local authorities or healthcare specialists. You may visit Tivoli with confidence if you put your health and safety first.

Dining and Entertainment

You may choose from a wide range of eating and entertainment choices in Tivoli to suit your likes and preferences. Here are some suggestions for places to eat and things to do in Tivoli at night:

- The ancient Ristorante Sibilla, which is located in the center of Tivoli, has a beautiful ambiance and serves typical Italian fare. It is renowned for its exquisite pastries, excellent seafood, and wonderful pasta meals. Savor the taste of genuine Italian food while having a romantic supper.

- The rustically decorated Trattoria Il Vecchio Mulino offers a comfortable atmosphere close to Villa d'Este. It specializes in regional cuisine, which includes grilled meats, handmade pasta, and decadent sweets. For the whole dining experience, drink some local wine with your meal.

- A combination of traditional and modern cuisine is served at Antica Osteria d'Este, a restaurant near Villa d'Este with a pleasant ambiance. It has a warm atmosphere and a deck for eating al fresco. Enjoy their large wine selection and their inventive takes on regional favorites.

- Piazza Garibaldi: Tivoli's central piazza comes alive at night with a variety of bustling cafés, pubs, and gelaterias. Enjoy a leisurely evening walk while indulging in gelato or espresso and taking in the energetic atmosphere.

- Wine Bars and Enotecas: There are several wine bars and enotecas in Tivoli where you may try a variety of local and Italian wines. These places are ideal for a laid-back evening of wine tasting and discussion since they often provide a comfortable and laid-back ambiance.

- Pubs & Bars: Tivoli has a few pubs and bars where you may have a drink or two if you're seeking a more laid-back evening experience. These places often include live music performances and provide a fun environment for mingling and relaxing.

Always double-check the opening times of the places you want to visit since they could change. Additionally, Tivoli may host regional festivals or events at certain periods of the year that provide distinctive eating and entertainment options. During your vacation, keep an eye out for any local events.

Every appetite and choice may be satisfied at Tivoli, whether you want gourmet cuisine, a casual dinner, or a buzzing nightlife.

Essential Travel Tips and Advice

It's always great to keep in mind a few important travel suggestions and advice while visiting Tivoli or any other location. Here are some ideas to improve the enjoyment of your visit to Tivoli:

- Plan your vacation and do your study about Tivoli's attractions, travel alternatives, regional traditions, and any unique rules or laws you should be aware of. Making the most of your time in Tivoli will be easier if you have a well-thought-out schedule.

- Check the weather prediction for Tivoli for the dates of your trip and prepare the proper clothes and footwear. Never leave home without such necessities as a good pair of walking shoes, a hat, sunscreen, and any required prescriptions.

- Learn Some Simple Local words: Being able to communicate with the locals and demonstrating respect for their culture will be made much easier by learning a few simple Italian words. "Hello," "Thank you," and "Excuse me" are common greetings and words that may leave a good impression.

- Respect Local Customs: Get to know Tivoli's regional traditions and customs.

Respect religious places, present yourself modestly while entering temples or churches, and observe any etiquette instructions at cultural icons.

- Keep yourself hydrated during the day, particularly in the warmer months, and carry snacks. Bring some nutritious snacks and a water bottle with you so you can stay energized while visiting Tivoli.

- Utilize Public transit: Tivoli has excellent access to buses and trains as well as other forms of public transit. Use these choices to go about the city and see the neighboring sights. Make sure to review the timetables and buy tickets as necessary.

- Pickpockets Should Stay Avoided: As in any tourist site, stay aware of your possessions and be on the lookout for pickpockets.

Avoid carrying significant amounts of cash, keep your valuables safe, and utilize hotel safes when they are available.

- Stay Connected: To stay online when traveling, think about getting a local SIM card or using roaming services. You can browse, do informational searches, and, if necessary, interact with people with the aid of the internet.

- While Tivoli is often a safe place to visit, it is advisable to use caution while out at night. Avoid dark passageways, stay in well-lit, busy places, and follow your gut.

- Travel insurance: Get travel insurance that pays for medical costs, trip cancellations, and other unexpected events to safeguard your goods and yourself. Verify that the policy addresses your unique requirements and activities.

Keep in mind that these suggestions are general counsel, so it's crucial to modify them for your unique travel circumstances. You should also heed any recommendations or instructions given by local authorities or the embassy or consulate of your nation. You may enjoy a wonderful and hassle-free vacation to Tivoli by being organized and educated.

Centers for Visitors Information and Resources

There are helpful contacts and tourist information centers at Tivoli that may aid you with any questions or requests for assistance. Here are a few important sources:

Tourist Information Office in Tivoli:

Location: Tivoli, Italy, Piazza Garibaldi, 2
Services: The tourist information office offers maps, brochures, and basic details on the sights, activities, and lodging in Tivoli. Additionally, they may provide you with advice on itineraries and respond to any special queries you may have.

Neighborhood Emergency Services

911 for emergencies
Officers: 113
Emergency Room Visits: 118
115 Fire Department

Embassies and consulates:

In case of an emergency or if help is required while you are in Italy, it is advised to have the embassy or consulate's phone number on hand.

Transporting People:

Tivoli Train Station: For information about trains, tickets, and getting to and from Tivoli.
Information about local bus routes, timetables, and prices is available under "Local Bus Services."

Accommodation Support

Your hotel or place of lodging may be a helpful source for information about the area, suggestions, and help with any problems or challenges you may have while there.

Online travel discussion boards, official Tivoli tourist websites, and smartphone travel apps may also provide more details and viewpoints from other visitors on their experiences in Tivoli.

If you need any help, advice, or information while you're in Tivoli, it's always a good idea to have these contacts close at hand.

Websites, Apps and Online Resources

There are several helpful websites and online resources that may provide helpful information and support while organizing your trip to Tivoli. These websites are suggested:

- The official tourist website of Tivoli offers information on the city's attractions, events, lodging options, transit options, and more. For the most recent information and resources, go to their website at www.visittivoli.eu.

- Travelers' reviews, ratings, and suggestions are available on TripAdvisor. In Tivoli, you can discover evaluations of tourist destinations, lodging options, dining establishments, and more to assist you in planning your trip. Please go to www.tripadvisor.com.

- Rome2rio is an excellent resource for organizing your travel from Rome or other locations to Tivoli. Along with projected journey times and prices, it offers alternatives for trains, buses, and other means of transportation. Please go to www.rome2rio.com.

- Official Websites of Attractions: For thorough information on opening hours, admission costs, guided tours, and any special events or exhibits, see the official websites of attractions like Villa d'Este and Hadrian's Villa (Villa Adriana). These websites often provide the most precise and recent information.

- Use online mapping tools like Google Maps or Apple Maps to find your way about Tivoli, identify places to visit, determine the best routes for using public transit, and make travel plans. You may view these maps on your computer or mobile device.

- Find travel blogs and forums that provide information, advice, and first-hand accounts from visitors who have been to Tivoli. These platforms may provide insider knowledge, undiscovered treasures, and useful guidance derived from actual experiences.

Keep in mind to cross-reference data from several sources to confirm its accuracy and applicability to your trip requirements. Additionally, it's a smart idea to look for any travel warnings or updates from the official government websites addressing security and health issues.

You may learn more, make plans for your trip, and get the most out of your time in Tivoli by making use of these online tools.

Tips for Language and Communication

It might be beneficial to bear in mind a few communication and linguistic hints whilst in Tivoli to improve your interactions with locals and improve your city navigation. Here are a few suggestions:

- Learn Some Basic Italian words: In Tivoli, knowing a few simple Italian words might be quite helpful. Simply saying "hello" (ciao) and "thank you" (grazie) may go a long way toward making a good first impression. Exclamations like "Excuse me" (scusa) and "Do you speak English?" (parli inglese?) may also be helpful when asking for help.

- Use Polite Language: When communicating with Italians, keep in mind to use the polite words "please" (per favore) and "thank you" (Grazie). Forging good relationships and getting help, politeness is very important.

- Carry a Phrasebook or Translation program: You may want to consider carrying a small phrasebook or downloading a translation program for your smartphone. When you need to search for words or phrases fast, these tools might be very useful if you have trouble communicating.

- Non-Verbal Communication: In Italian culture, non-verbal cues like body language and gestures may be quite important. Be aware of your nonverbal clues and respect regional traditions. For instance, Italians often accentuate their phrases with hand gestures; but, if you are unfamiliar with their precise connotations, it is wise to refrain from overdoing it.

- Patience and a Smile: Be patient and courteous while interacting with Tivoli residents. Even if you don't speak the language well, a grin may ease tension and foster a friendly environment. If locals observe your effort and cheerful attitude, they will often offer to help or use another method of communication.

- Use Visual Aids: If you face language challenges, think about asking for instructions or expressing your requirements using visual aids. When verbal communication is scarce, pointing to a map, displaying an image, or utilizing hand gestures might be useful communication methods.

- Look for Locals Who Speak English: You're more likely to encounter locals who speak English or other widely spoken languages in tourist areas or institutions. If you need support in English, don't be afraid to contact hotel workers, staff at tourist information centers, or members of the service sector for help.

Keep in mind that not all people may speak English well, particularly in more rural or undeveloped regions. However, you may overcome language obstacles and forge lasting relationships in Tivoli by making an effort to learn a few fundamental words and approaching encounters with respect and a cheerful attitude.

Basic Helpful Phrases

Hello: Ciao (chow)

Good morning: Buongiorno (bwon jor-no)

Good evening: Buonasera (bwon-a-se-ra)

Goodbye: Arrivederci

(a-ree-veh-dehr-chee)

Please: Per favore (per fa-vo-re)

Thank you: Grazie (gra-tzee-eh)

You're welcome: Prego (preh-go)

Excuse me: Scusa (scoo-za) or Mi scusi

(mee scoo-zee)

Yes: Sì (see)

No: No (no)

I don't understand: Non capisco (non

ka-pee-skoh)

Do you speak English?: Parli inglese?

(par-lee een-gle-seh?)

I'm sorry: Mi dispiace (mee

dee-spee-ah-che)

How much does it cost?: Quanto costa?

(kwahn-toh co-sta?)

Where is...?: Dove si trova...? (do-veh see

tro-va...?)

Can you help me?: Puoi aiutarmi? (pwoy

eye-oo-tar-mee?)

I need a doctor: Ho bisogno di un dottore

(oh bee-so-nyoh dee oon dot-to-re)

Where is the restroom?: Dove si trova il

bagno? (do-veh see tro-va eel ba-nyo?)

Cheers!: Salute! (sa-loo-teh)

Have a nice day: Buona giornata (bwon-a

jor-na-ta)

When utilizing these expressions, keep in mind to talk slowly and clearly. You should also feel free to utilize gestures or other visual cues to help communicate. Even if you just know a few basic words, the locals will appreciate your attempt to speak with them in Italian.

Money and Budgeting Tips

- Italy uses the Euro (EUR) as its official currency. Before traveling to Tivoli, make sure you have some euros on hand since this is the preferred currency for most transactions.

- ATMs and currency exchange: You may use your debit or credit card to withdraw cash at Tivoli's ATMs (bancomats). To avoid paying high fees, seek reputed banks or ATMs connected to significant financial institutions. If you need to convert foreign money into euros, you may also locate currency exchange facilities in the city.

- Credit Cards: In Tivoli, particularly at hotels, eateries, and bigger institutions, credit cards are routinely accepted. To be safe, it's a good idea to have extra cash on hand for smaller shops, neighborhood markets, or other establishments that may not take cards.

- Establish your spending limit for Tivoli's lodging, food, transportation, attractions, and shopping. To help you budget your spending effectively, do some prior research on the typical prices of these things. Consider setting up a separate budget for mementos or unforeseen costs.

- Tivoli provides a variety of eating alternatives to suit all budgets. You may choose from options that meet your budget, such as expensive eateries and informal trattorias. Consider eating at neighborhood cafés or sampling some of the city's delectable street cuisine to save money.

- Tipping is not required in Italy since a service fee is often tacked on to the tab at restaurants. However, as a sign of gratitude for exceptional service, it's customary to offer a little tip (often between 5 and 10% of the whole amount).

- Water: Consider bringing a refillable water bottle and filling it up at drinking fountains or asking for tap water in restaurants rather than purchasing bottled water. The excellent tap water in Italy can keep you hydrated and save you money.

- Tivoli includes several free or inexpensive attractions, including open-air parks, gardens, and specific vistas. Utilize these choices to discover the city on a budget and yet appreciate its beauty.

- Shopping & Souvenirs: Tivoli has a variety of souvenir stores where you may buy distinctive regional arts, crafts, and specialty goods. To make sure you're getting the greatest deal possible, set a budget for souvenirs and check costs at several shops.

- Travel insurance: Put your health and safety first by acquiring travel insurance that pays for unexpected costs like medical bills and trip cancellations. To understand what is covered and if you may need extra coverage, thoroughly review the policy.

XI. TIVOLI VACATION ITINERARY

Day 1: Getting to know Villa d'Este and its neighborhood

Morning:

- Visit the UNESCO World Heritage Site noted for its beautiful gardens and fountains, Villa d'Este, first thing in the morning. Investigate the villa's interior, which has exquisite architecture and lovely paintings.

- Enjoy the beautiful sculptures, terraces, and water features as you leisurely meander around the grounds. Enjoy Tivoli's serene ambiance and breathtaking vistas.

Afternoon:

- Visit the adjacent Ristorante Sibilla for a relaxing lunch after your tour of Villa d'Este. This historic eatery provides delectable Italian food, including regional specialties, in a picturesque setting.

- Take a little stroll to see Tivoli's old town after lunch. Admire the Cathedral of San Lorenzo's architecture while strolling around the charming Piazza del Plebiscito.

Evening:

- Enjoy a leisurely meal at one of Tivoli's neighborhood trattorias as the day comes to a close. Try some of the classic Roman meals like saltimbocca alla Romana, cacio e pepe, and carbonara.

- Take a walk around Tivoli's streets to wind down the evening and take in the atmosphere of the town after dark. Grab a scoop of gelato from one of the gelaterias and enjoy the delectable flavors while seeing Tivoli's beautifully lit streets.

Note: Be careful to research the Villa d'Este's opening hours and any reservations needed in advance. It is advised to buy tickets in advance to prevent lengthy lines, particularly during the busiest travel times.

Day 2: Visiting Villa Adriana and surrounding sites

Morning:

- Visit Villa Adriana, commonly referred to as Hadrian's Villa, which is situated close to Tivoli, first thing in the morning. Investigate the huge structure that once housed the opulent palace of Emperor Hadrian.

- Visit the location on your own or with a guide, and be amazed by the well-preserved remains of temples, spas, theaters, and other buildings. Don't overlook the magnificent Canopus, a reflecting pool encircled by columns that evoke Egyptian design.

Afternoon:

- Lunch on a picnic blanket in the serene grounds of Villa Adriana. Find a space in the shade and unwind while admiring the picturesque surroundings and the calm mood.

- Make your way to the neighboring Temple of Vesta after lunch. This circular temple is in excellent condition and provides beautiful picture possibilities as well as an insight into the design of early Roman architecture.

Evening:

- In the evening, go back to Tivoli and spend some time seeing some of the town's lesser-known sights. Via della Sibilla is a wonderful street surrounded by old structures and attractive stores. Take a leisurely walk along it.

- Visit the Tivoli Historical Museum to see the collection of objects from Villa Adriana and other historical sites and to expand your knowledge of the region's rich history.

- Enjoy a leisurely meal at one of Tivoli's neighborhood trattorias or eateries to round off your day of discovery as you appreciate genuine Italian fare.

You'll be spending a lot of the day outside, so make sure to pack sunscreen and wear comfortable walking shoes. Bring a bottle of water and some food for the day's activities as well.

Day 3: Local immersion and adventures off the beaten path

Morning:

- Start your day by visiting Tivoli's less well-known areas off the beaten tourist trail. Take a stroll around the neighborhoods to see the unique architecture, quaint streets, and individuals going about their daily lives.

- Visit the neighborhood market, Mercato di Tivoli, where you can take in the lively ambiance and find a range of fresh food, regional specialties, and handcrafted goods. Take part in the conversations with the sellers and possibly buy some supplies for a picnic later in the day.

Afternoon:

- Drive to the small town of Subiaco, which is tucked away in the Aniene Valley. Visit the Monastery of St. Benedict, a prominent spiritual and cultural destination, and stroll around the city's medieval center. Explore the Sacro Speco, and the cave church, and take in the breathtaking paintings.

- Indulge in a leisurely meal of customary fare and regional delicacies at a neighborhood trattoria in Subiaco.

Evening:

- Return to Tivoli and take in a live show or concert to experience the local culture. If there are any performances of music or theater happening while you are there, check the schedule at Villa d'Este or other locations.

- As an alternative, think about enrolling in a cooking class or wine-tasting event to discover Italian food and savor regional tastes.

Note: Check the opening times and activity availability in advance since they could change based on the time of year and day of the week. At all times of the day, embrace the spirit of exploration and have an open mind to unexpected discoveries.

XII. CONCLUSION

Final thoughts on Tivoli as a Tourism Destination

A pleasant vacation experience that incorporates history, art, scenic beauty, and regional character is provided by Tivoli. It has a lot to offer as a resort, from the opulence of Villa Adriana to the charming gardens and fountains of Villa d'Este. There are options for off-the-beaten-path exploration and a deeper engagement in the community at Tivoli's lesser-known attractions and hidden jewels.

The town's charming streets, historic district, and bustling markets provide a window into daily life in Tivoli. The town's traditions are given a dynamic atmosphere by the yearly festivals and cultural events, and the gastronomic scene offers the opportunity to savor genuine Italian food.

Tivoli won't let you down whether you're a history buff, a nature lover, or an inquisitive traveler looking for uncommon encounters. Due to its proximity to Rome, it provides for a wonderful day trip or a tranquil retreat from the busy city. A remarkable vacation experience is produced by the region's stunning scenery and rich historical and cultural history.

When organizing your trip to Tivoli, take into account visiting the well-known sites as well as setting aside time to explore the undiscovered sights and mingle with the people.

Take advantage of the chance to interact with the locals and enjoy the true charm of this Italian treasure while immersing yourself in the history, architecture, and natural beauty that Tivoli has to offer.

Encouragement to Discover Lazio's Hidden Gems

Go out on an adventure of exploration and discovery to find Lazio's undiscovered gems. Although the area is sometimes overshadowed by well-known locations, it has a variety of jewels that are just waiting to be discovered.

Expand your horizons and you'll be rewarded with enthralling experiences. Discover the quaint rural towns and villages where time has seemed to stand still. Explore the quaint neighborhoods, take in the culture, and interact with the welcoming locals who represent the best of Italian hospitality.

Learn about the Roman ruins that date back thousands of years. Admire the exquisite mosaics, spectacular amphitheaters, and historically accurate constructions that have been meticulously conserved. Explore Lazio's rich legacy and history, and see the tales come to life before your eyes.

Experience the natural splendor of the area, from the vineyards and rolling hills to the tranquil lakes and rocky shoreline. Hike along beautiful paths, take in the clean air, and take in the stunning views that will astound you.

Treat your taste buds to some of the area's gastronomic treats. Lazio is recognized for its wonderful cuisine, which includes classic pasta dishes, scrumptious cheeses, and renowned wines. Discover regional markets, eat at family-run trattorias, and enjoy the genuine tastes that highlight the area's culinary history.

Step off the established route and into uncharted territory without fear. Let Lazio's hidden gems take you by surprise; there are fresh adventures to be had around every curve. Lazio will enchant you with its subtle beauty and undiscovered tales, whether you're looking for peace, cultural immersion, or just a change of pace.

So, have a curious and open mind as you go on. Allow Lazio to disclose its mysteries and charm you with its buried riches. Embrace the adventure since the true spirit of travel can only be discovered by exploring uncharted territory. Enjoy the Adventure!

Made in the USA
Monee, IL
09 February 2024